YAS

11/02

W9-BAZ-940

The Library of
Political Assassinations

The Assassination of
Martin Luther King Jr.

Jacqueline Ching

The Rosen Publishing Group, Inc.
New York

Published in 2002 by The Rosen Publishing Group, Inc.
29 East 21st Street, New York, NY 10010

First Edition

Library of Congress Cataloging-in-Publication Data

Ching, Jacqueline.
The assassination of Martin Luther King Jr. / by Jacqueline Ching.
p. cm. — (The library of political assassinations)
Includes bibliographical references and index.
Summary: Examines the life and death of Martin Luther King Jr., his impact on society, his assassination, and his legacy as a slain African American hero.
ISBN 0-8239-3543-4 (library binding)
1. King, Martin Luther, Jr., 1929–1968—Assassination—Juvenile literature. [1. King, Martin Luther, Jr., 1929–1968—Assassination. 2. Civil rights workers. 3. Clergy. 4. African Americans— Biography.]
I. Title. II. Series.
E185.97.K5 C47 2002
323'.092—dc21

2001003455

Manufactured in the United States of America

(*Previous page*) Martin Luther King Jr. greets the crowd at the Lincoln Memorial during his "I Have a Dream" speech at the civil rights march on Washington, D.C., on August 28, 1963.

Contents

The tomb of civil rights leader Martin Luther King Jr. stands amid a decorative pool in the Freedom Hall complex in Atlanta, Georgia.

Introduction

Martin Luther King Jr. became one of the most important leaders of the civil rights movement, inspired a generation, and helped to change American society. The civil rights movement began in the 1950s when African Americans organized to protest racial segregation in the South. It gained momentum in the 1960s, a decade in which King also attained national recognition.

The civil rights movement challenged the existence of prejudice based on race, sex, religion, or national origin. King and his followers questioned an America that treated African Americans as second-class citizens. In so doing, they took issue with the beliefs of those in authority. Not surprisingly, such a challenge met with strong resistance and resulted in angry and often violent confrontations.

After the Civil War ended in the second half of the nineteenth century, during a period called the Reconstruction, white lawmakers in the South passed laws segregating, or legally separating, blacks and whites. These laws were called Jim Crow laws. "Jump Jim Crow" was the name of a minstrel act first performed in 1828. As a result, the term "Jim Crow" became a negative term, especially for African Americans, as it referred to segregation. Early Jim Crow laws required that "persons of color" and whites be separated in public places, including trains, restaurants, schools, and parks. "Persons of color" referred to anyone even suspected of having African ancestry.

During the civil rights movement, an organization called the National Association for the Advancement of Colored People (NAACP) succeeded in winning a number of important court cases that challenged Jim Crow laws. One of their most important victories was the 1954 decision *Brown v. Board of Education*. In this case, the Supreme Court finally ruled that segregation in public schools was unconstitutional, or illegal.

Other rulings against Jim Crow laws soon followed, protecting the rights of all citizens, black or white, as established in the Constitution of the United States. But the new legislation was far from able to change conditions overnight. It took the continued efforts of civil rights leaders and groups to enact social change.

By 1960, peaceful sit-ins, patterned on the technique of Mohandas Gandhi, leader of the movement to end British rule in India, became a common protest strategy. Soon, African Americans throughout the South, including Dr. King, were holding sit-ins in response to racial segregation at cafeterias, libraries, beaches, and even churches. When protesters were arrested, the NAACP joined King to defend them and also provide assistance in holding the sit-ins.

Early in his career as a freedom fighter, Martin Luther King Jr. focused on segregation, especially in the South. After several victories, King turned his attention to fighting for voting rights. Although according to the law African Americans had the right to vote, local officials often developed requirements that prevented African Americans from exercising that right.

After the Voting Rights Act was signed into law in 1965, King focused on economic problems, such as poor housing and a lack of job opportunities, which even affected African Americans in northern cities. Through all of this, he never wavered from his policy of nonviolence.

King's commitment to nonviolence stemmed from his belief that African Americans could never win a violent confrontation against armed authorities. But this commitment was not only a practical one. He condemned violence as immoral. At the center of his philosophy was the belief that people tend to choose good over evil. Through nonviolent protest, he hoped to make injustices visible by forcing the oppressor to see the pain of the oppressed. King's approach was revolutionary. He insisted on peaceful protest, arguing that "nonviolence is the most potent technique for oppressed people."

Although King and his followers took this peaceful approach, their opponents, including the police, did not, and peaceful demonstrations often ended in riots and arrests. Even some of the people King hoped to represent found nonviolent protest neither an easy nor a logical approach. African Americans and poor people, who had long been frustrated and humiliated, were not always willing to turn the other cheek. King understood that he would have to repeatedly defend his nonviolent approach.

King was imprisoned several times for following his conscience. In 1963, King and other ministers were arrested after a demonstration to protest the segregation of public facilities in Birmingham, Alabama. While in prison, King wrote his famous "Letter from Birmingham Jail," explaining the need for nonviolent civil disobedience: "There comes a time when a moral man can't obey a law which his conscience tells him is unjust."

In the later years of his life, King sought to form a coalition of poor people of all races. This coalition would address such economic problems as poverty and unemployment. His efforts along these lines, however, did not generate as much support as his earlier campaigns. Nevertheless, he planned for a Poor People's Campaign march to Washington, D.C.; King planned to walk with 3,000 of the nation's poor to demand sweeping legislation to fight poverty.

These plans were interrupted in the spring of 1968 by a trip to Memphis, Tennessee. King traveled there to show his support for a strike by that city's sanitation workers. On April 4, he was killed by a sniper's bullet while standing on the balcony of the Lorraine Motel.

The Assassination

Having waged a nonviolent battle for civil rights for over two dozen years, by 1968 Martin Luther King Jr. decided on a new campaign. He had challenged segregation in the South and enabled thousands of African Americans to register to vote. Now he began to organize the Poor People's Campaign.

He planned to march in Washington, D.C., to demand sweeping legislation to fight poverty. People of every race and creed were invited to join in. Organizers also planned to build a city of shacks within sight of the White House and the Capitol. It was a class-based march that would cross racial divisions.

But the need to support striking African American sanitation workers in Memphis, Tennessee, interrupted these plans. On January 31, 1968, sanitation workers were sent home because of rain. African American workers were paid for only two hours that day, while white workers were paid for the entire day. African American workers went on strike. They demanded higher wages and better working conditions. When their demands were ignored, they called for a work stoppage. The leaders of the strike asked for Dr. King's support.

A Peaceful Protest Turns Violent

Dr. King and the workers planned a demonstration on March 28, 1968. On the morning of the demonstration, peaceful marchers walked with banners that read "I Am a Man." The leaders of the strike had promised Dr. King that a group of militant African American activists known as the Invaders would not be part of the march. However, when King arrived, they were among the peaceful marchers and soon changed the tone of the demonstration.

Striking African American sanitation workers in Memphis, Tennessee, were met by National Guard tanks.

Members of the Invaders dropped out of line and started breaking store windows and looting, or stealing. King called for the march to be stopped immediately. His long-time friend Reverend James Lawson announced over a bullhorn, "Disperse. Please go to your homes." King's followers, who were committed to nonviolence, left peacefully. But other demonstrators continued to loot.

A police officer beats a youth with his nightstick during the looting that ensued after the breakup of the Memphis sanitation workers' strike.

During the disorder that followed the march, police shot a sixteen-year-old African American youth. Sixty others were clubbed and wounded, and 280 people were arrested. The looting and arson continued until the governor of Tennessee ordered 4,000 National Guardsmen to the scene.

King returned to Atlanta, Georgia, shaken by the incident. Although he had not planned the demonstration, he felt responsible for its results. He was determined to show that nonviolence could still bring about desired social change. So he planned a second march in Memphis for Monday, April 8, 1968.

The Second Trip to Memphis

A number of Dr. King's supporters wanted him to give up on Memphis and focus on the Poor People's Campaign. Memphis officials also tried to prevent the second demonstration from taking place by obtaining a court injunction, declaring that the march would endanger public safety. Nevertheless, Dr. King announced his intention to successfully lead a peaceful demonstration.

King arrived in Memphis on April 3, 1968. That night, because of heavy rain, he expected only a small crowd at a rally at Mason Temple, where he planned to speak. Two thousand people showed up. Addressing the audience, he said that he had heard talk of threats on his life. In response he said, "Like anybody, I would like to live a long life . . . Longevity has its place. But I'm not concerned about that now. I just want to do God's will. And He's allowed me to go up to the mountain. And I've looked over, and I've seen the promised land. I may not get there with you, but I want you to know tonight that we as a people will get to the promised land. So I'm happy tonight."

The Lorraine Motel

While in Memphis, Dr. King and several associates checked into the Lorraine Motel on Mulberry Street. Dr. King's room, #306, was on the second floor, facing

The Rev. Martin Luther King Jr. stands with other civil rights leaders on the balcony of the Lorraine Motel in Memphis, Tennessee, on April 3, 1968, the day before he was assassinated at the same place. From left to right are Hosea Williams, Jesse Jackson, King, and Ralph Abernathy.

Mulberry Street. His room had a door that opened onto a balcony directly above the motel's parking lot. Across from the motel on Mulberry Street was a back-yard area of buildings whose fronts faced South Main Street. South Main and Mulberry Streets ran parallel to one another. Fire Station No. 2 faced South Main Street and was located at the end of the block between South Main and Mulberry Streets.

A fenced-in parking area was next to the fire station on South Main Street. Next to that was Canipe's, a record store, and Jim's Grill, a tavern. Directly above Jim's Grill, on the second floor, was a

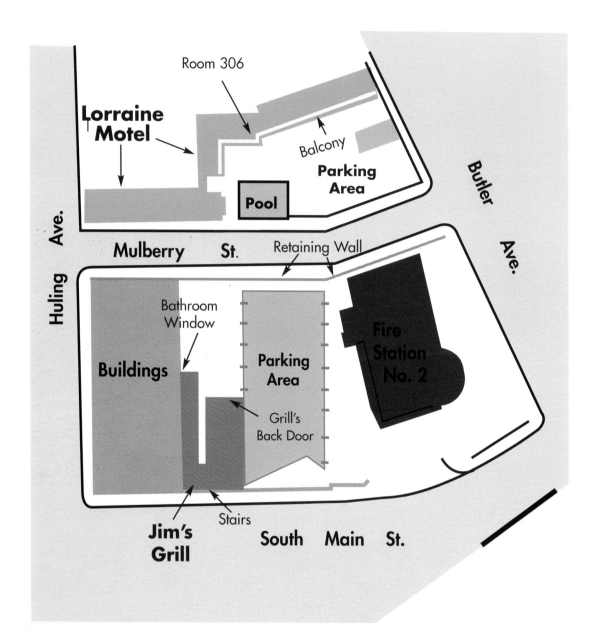

Room 306

Lorraine
Motel

Balcony

Parking
Area

Pool

Butler

Mulberry   St.   Retaining Wall

Huling

Ave.

Ave.

Bathroom
Window

Buildings

Parking
Area

Fire
Station
No. 2

Grill's
Back Door

Jim's
Grill

Stairs

South   Main   St.

This is a diagram of the Lorraine Motel, where Martin Luther King Jr. was assassinated, and the surrounding area.

rooming house. Loyd Jowers owned and operated Jim's Grill. After 4:00 PM, Jowers generally worked alone or with one other person. The back door to Jim's Grill opened to backyards that overlooked Mulberry Street and the Lorraine Motel.

Sometime before 4:00 PM on April 4, 1968, James Earl Ray parked his white Mustang on South Main Street and, under an assumed name, John Willard, checked into the rooming house above Jim's Grill. Ray was first shown a room at the front looking out onto South Main Street, but asked for room 5-B instead, which was located at the back of the house and faced the Lorraine Motel.

This is the view from the window in Memphis, Tennessee, from which a man fired a gun, fatally wounding Martin Luther King Jr.

Ray's room was on the second floor of the rooming house. Both that room and the communal bathroom at the end of the hall had windows overlooking Dr. King's motel room. Shortly after renting the room, Ray purchased binoculars from a nearby store and then returned to the rooming house.

King had spent most of the day with his aides inside his motel room. They organized the planned march down to the last detail. That evening, he prepared for dinner with Reverend Ralph Abernathy and Reverend Samuel Kyles. They went out on the balcony, which overlooked the parking lot. Below them, other demonstration organizers gathered around the white Cadillac that had come for King. The driver shouted to him to bring a coat, as it was getting cold. King asked Abernathy to get one for him.

Civil rights leader Andrew Young *(left)* and others on the balcony of the Lorraine Motel point toward the shooter after the assassination of Martin Luther King Jr., who lies at their feet.

A Sniper's Shot

Just before 6:00 PM, Dr. King was outside on the balcony of the Lorraine Motel in front of his room. From the balcony, King saw Ben Branch, a musician from Chicago, standing with his associate Jesse Jackson. He asked Branch to play "Precious Lord, Take My Hand" at a second rally scheduled at the Mason Temple that night. "Sing it real pretty," King said. Suddenly, a shot rang out. From the bathroom window of the rooming house, a sniper's single shot from a high-powered rifle struck and threw King back onto the concrete balcony. He was rushed to a hospital. An hour later, the man who had influenced and inspired so many was dead at age thirty-nine.

Freedom Fighter

On January 15, 1929, a son was born to the Reverend and Alberta Williams King of Atlanta, Georgia. The couple named their first son Martin after Reverend King. He was called M.L. by his family. King's childhood home was located in a residential section of Atlanta known as Sweet Auburn. Two blocks away stood the church where M.L.'s father was pastor, Ebenezer Baptist Church.

As a student, Martin Luther King Jr. excelled in school. Because of his high score on the college entrance exams in his junior year of high school, King advanced to Morehouse College without formally graduating from Booker T. Washington High School. As he had skipped both the ninth and twelfth grades, King entered Morehouse at the age of fifteen.

King entered the Christian ministry and was ordained at his father's church in February 1948. At the age of nineteen, following his ordination, he also became the assistant pastor of Ebenezer Baptist Church. In 1951, he entered Boston University for graduate study.

In 1953, King married Coretta Scott and settled in Montgomery, Alabama. There, he became pastor of the Dexter Avenue Baptist Church. He had a small congregation, but among the worshipers were many of the city's most influential African American citizens. In 1955, King completed his graduate work and received a Ph.D. in theology from Boston University.

The Montgomery Bus Boycott

That same year, Dr. King first gained national attention during the boycott to protest segregated public buses in Montgomery, Alabama. Prior to the boycott, the front seats of city buses were reserved for whites, while the back was reserved for African Americans. Rosa Parks, an African American woman, was sitting in the whites-only section of the bus and refused to give up her seat to a white passenger. The police arrested Parks, who was a respected citizen of the community. Civic leaders and local ministers, including King, went into action. They met at the Dexter Avenue Baptist Church to discuss a plan.

A sheriff fingerprints Rosa Parks after she refused to give up her seat on a bus to a white passenger. Parks's action led to a boycott of buses, which in turn led to the U.S. Supreme Court decision that all segregation is unlawful.

They decided to boycott the buses the following Monday, the same day that Rosa Parks was scheduled to go on trial. Parks was found guilty and fined $14 for disobeying the segregation law. The boycott went into effect and was highly successful, in part because African Americans made up 70 percent of bus riders in Montgomery.

Since the boycott was televised, the world witnessed the protests. It became a turning point in the civil rights movement. The boycott lasted over a year, ending on November 13, 1956, when the U.S. Supreme Court upheld a lower court's decision declaring Montgomery's segregated seating unconstitutional.

The Southern Christian Leadership Conference

On the heels of the boycott, King held a meeting of sixty African American leaders, mostly ministers, at his father's church in Atlanta. The meeting resulted in a new organization, the Southern Christian Leadership Conference (SCLC). The leaders elected King president, a position he held until his death.

The founders of the SCLC wanted to build on the success of the Montgomery bus boycott. They hoped to sweep the South with mass nonviolent protests. But there were more obstacles to overcome.

Martin Luther King Jr. *(center)* and Reverend Ralph Abernathy *(left)* are arrested by Albany chief of police Laurie Pritchett *(right)* during a civil rights protest at the Albany, Georgia, city hall.

King and the SCLC helped to secure the right to vote for many African Americans. In 1961, during a voter registration campaign in Albany, Georgia, police jailed 471 African Americans because they wanted to vote. King and his friend Reverend Ralph Abernathy arrived on the scene in December to boost morale.

The next day, December 16, 1961, King and Abernathy led 250 African American marchers from the church to city hall, where the police were waiting. When protesters refused to disband, they were arrested. Dr. King was jailed after refusing to pay a fine for organizing the march. King went to jail and successfully drew attention to the injustice of the situation.

Dr. King was also jailed after he led another march on Albany's city hall in July 1962. Unfortunately, none of this helped the Albany movement, which ultimately lost steam. Disappointed, King decided that the problem of racism had to be dramatized in a bigger way.

Birmingham

King traveled to Birmingham, Alabama, a city that was known as a fortress of white supremacy, with one of the meanest police forces in the country. On April 3, 1963, Dr. King issued the "Birmingham Manifesto." In it, he demanded jobs for African Americans and the desegregation of public facilities.

On April 12, Dr. King and Rev. Abernathy led a group of fifty marchers to Birmingham city hall. As expected, police arrested and jailed the protesters. King was sent into solitary confinement, where he sat alone in a bare and empty cell. Police did not permit King to see visitors or make phone calls for a full day.

Coretta Scott King contacted the White House and President John F. Kennedy for assistance. She also hoped to draw attention to the situation. The SCLC made sure to spread the word that President Kennedy was looking into the matter personally.

Meanwhile, as he waited to be released from prison, King wrote a response to an appeal written by eight Birmingham clergy urging African Americans not to participate in demonstrations.

His "Letter from Birmingham Jail" explained the need for nonviolent demonstrations and criticized whites for disobeying the Supreme Court's desegregation decision of 1954.

To raise the stakes even further, Dr. King urged young people to become involved in the movement. With the help of Rev. James Bevel, African American students were trained in nonviolent protest. On May 2, 1963, they began to march and sing freedom songs. They were soon arrested. Later, King was criticized for risking the lives of children in the protest.

Civil rights leader Martin Luther King Jr. strikes a contemplative pose as he sits in a jail cell in the Jefferson County Courthouse in Birmingham, Alabama.

However, the march could not have been more successful in terms of attracting national press coverage. More than a thousand strong, the students were arrested, filling the city's prisons. Police brutality was widely documented in pictures. Photos revealed crushing streams of water being aimed at the protesters from fire trucks, knocking them to the ground.

An Unjust Law

This is an excerpt from King's "Letter from Birmingham Jail," 1963:

One may well ask: "How can you advocate breaking some laws and obeying others?" The answer lies in the fact that there are two types of laws: just and unjust. I would be the first to advocate obeying just laws. One has not only a legal but a moral responsibility to obey just laws. Conversely, one has a moral responsibility to disobey unjust laws. I would agree with St. Augustine that "an unjust law is no law at all."

As a result, President Kennedy could no longer ignore the situation. He sent the head of the civil rights division of the Department of Justice (the government agency responsible for enforcing criminal laws), Burke Marshall, to Birmingham. Finally, on May 10, an agreement was reached and a truce was called. Birmingham's white business owners promised to desegregate lunch counters, rest rooms, and other public places; to hire African Americans; and to establish a channel of communication between African Americans and whites. The Birmingham campaign was a victory for Dr. King and a great moment for the civil rights movement.

Following the agreement, an attempt was made on King's life. Someone bombed Dr. King's headquarters at the Gaston Motel in Birmingham. Fortunately, King had already returned to Atlanta.

March on Washington

On August 28, 1963, the largest civil rights demonstration in the United States was held in Washington, D.C. The purpose of the march

Former Brooklyn Dodgers baseball star Jackie Robinson *(right)* and former heavyweight boxing champion Floyd Patterson examine bomb damage at a motel in Birmingham, Alabama, on May 14, 1963. Both came to Birmingham to speak at a rally for integration.

was to put moral pressure on the national government to pass civil rights legislation. More than 250,000 peaceful protesters gathered at the Lincoln Memorial to hear Dr. King speak.

At the demonstration, King shared his vision of the future of race relations in the United States. He said, "I have a dream that one day this nation will rise up and live out the true meaning of its creed: 'We hold these truths to be self-evident, that all men are created equal.' " To the cheering crowd, he

Dr. Martin Luther King Jr. delivers his famous "I Have a Dream" speech in front of the Lincoln Memorial during the Freedom March on Washington, D.C., on August 28, 1963.

described a land where whites and blacks would live as brothers, and where his people would be able to sing, "Free at last! Free at last! Thank God Almighty, we are free at last!"

Before his assassination in November 1963, President Kennedy had lobbied for the Civil Rights Act to be passed. Finally, in July 1964, it was signed into law by Kennedy's successor, President Lyndon B. Johnson. Senators from the South had failed to stop the passage of the bill that was meant to end discrimination based on race, sex, religion, or national origin. However, confrontations between blacks and whites continued.

In fact, other powerful voices had emerged within the African American community. Some questioned whether the nonviolent civil rights movement was actually serving their needs. Malcolm X had also emerged as an African American leader during the 1960s. He voiced black pride and initially called for separatism and the creation of a black nation. He also advocated violence as a means of self-defense. Before his assassination in 1965, Malcolm X seemed to embody African American defiance of white supremacy. After his death, Malcolm X became a hero to an increasing number of African Americans.

Man of the Year

In 1964, King was awarded the Nobel Peace Prize, an honor he took very seriously. The Nobel Prizes are the highest honors in the world awarded for intellectual achievement. Also in 1964, *Time* magazine named Dr. King Man of the Year. King then focused on another major issue: voting rights for African Americans. Although African Americans legally possessed the right to vote, few actually could.

Throughout the South, whites used violent intimidation tactics to keep African Americans out of polling booths. Often, voting officials forced African Americans to take a literacy test before allowing them to vote. In some places, the Ku Klux Klan (a violent white supremacist organization) terrorized African Americans who attempted to vote.

In 1964, *Time* magazine named Dr. King its Man of the Year.

King and the SCLC decided to center their voting rights campaign on the town of Selma, Alabama. They chose Selma mainly because the town's white citizens made up 99 percent of voters but were only slightly less than 50 percent of the population. Of the 15,000 African Americans in Selma, only 383 were registered to vote. Initially, the demonstrations remained peaceful. No one wanted to repeat the violent scenes of Birmingham. African Americans lined up in an orderly fashion outside the courthouse to register to vote, but after waiting for hours, they were told that the office was closed.

To protest this unfair treatment, King organized a march starting from Selma and ending at the state capitol building in Montgomery. Although he planned the march, King did not lead it. The marchers were turned back by state troopers with

nightsticks and tear gas. King personally led a
second march, but the group of 1,500 marchers,
black and white, were stopped by a wall of state
troopers. Instead of going on and forcing a confrontation, King and his followers knelt in prayer
and then unexpectedly
turned back.

Nevertheless, news
of the drama in Selma
spread around the
country and placed
enough pressure on
Congress to pass the
Voting Rights Act of
1965. The act allowed
the attorney general, the
chief law officer of the
nation, to enforce the
registration of African
American voters and to
end the use of literacy
tests and other devices
that had prevented
African Americans from
voting. As a result, the
number of registered

Private citizens and law enforcement
officials harassed and terrorized civil
rights protesters marching from
Selma to Montgomery, Alabama.
Nevertheless, the march succeeded
in pressuring Congress to pass the
Voting Rights Act of 1965.

African American voters, along with the number of
African Americans holding elective offices, increased
drastically in the South.

The Life of Dr. Martin Luther King Jr.

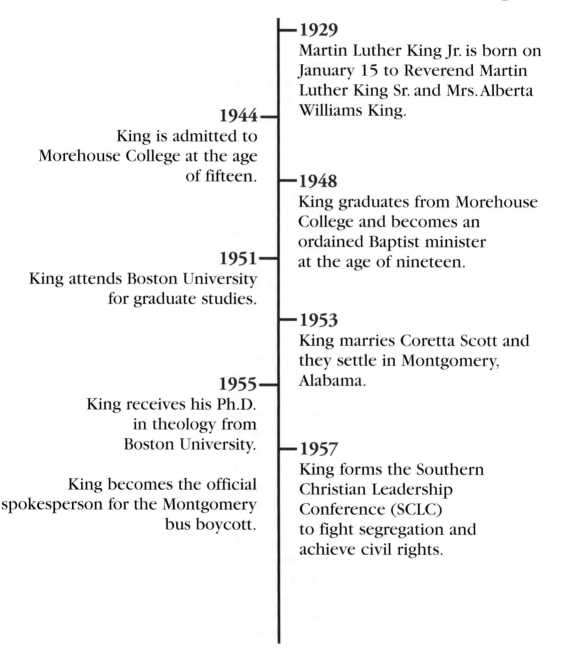

1929
Martin Luther King Jr. is born on January 15 to Reverend Martin Luther King Sr. and Mrs. Alberta Williams King.

1944
King is admitted to Morehouse College at the age of fifteen.

1948
King graduates from Morehouse College and becomes an ordained Baptist minister at the age of nineteen.

1951
King attends Boston University for graduate studies.

1953
King marries Coretta Scott and they settle in Montgomery, Alabama.

1955
King receives his Ph.D. in theology from Boston University.

King becomes the official spokesperson for the Montgomery bus boycott.

1957
King forms the Southern Christian Leadership Conference (SCLC) to fight segregation and achieve civil rights.

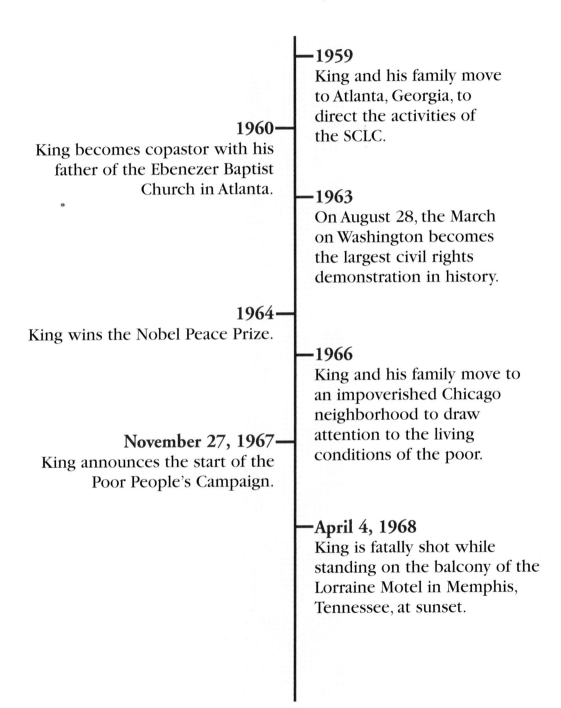

1959
King and his family move to Atlanta, Georgia, to direct the activities of the SCLC.

1960
King becomes copastor with his father of the Ebenezer Baptist Church in Atlanta.

1963
On August 28, the March on Washington becomes the largest civil rights demonstration in history.

1964
King wins the Nobel Peace Prize.

1966
King and his family move to an impoverished Chicago neighborhood to draw attention to the living conditions of the poor.

November 27, 1967
King announces the start of the Poor People's Campaign.

April 4, 1968
King is fatally shot while standing on the balcony of the Lorraine Motel in Memphis, Tennessee, at sunset.

Poverty

The victories won by Dr. King and the civil rights movement were significant, but they also revealed how far American society still had to go in terms of achieving true social equality. King began to realize that the civil rights movement had focused on integration but not on the serious economic inequalities in America, especially between African Americans and whites in urban areas.

King wanted to address the problem of poverty in African American ghettos, areas within a city where members of a minority group are forced to live because of legal, economic, and/or social pressure. In January 1966, King moved his family to a poor neighborhood in Chicago, Illinois, to draw attention to the living conditions of the poor. On July 10, King began a nonviolent campaign to end discrimination in housing, employment, and schools in Chicago.

While white city leaders opposed King's efforts, King also met with resistance from within the African American community. Some African Americans had become impatient with King's nonviolent tactics. Change came too slowly; African Americans had endured inequality and injustice for too long, and they called for more aggressive or militant measures.

Conservative black leaders also began to criticize King. They wanted him to stop the marches in and around Chicago, which they felt solved nothing and instead created racial tension. To prevent further violence, King and other civil rights leaders met with the mayor of Chicago, Richard Daley, and representatives of the business community. They reached an agreement, but city officials never honored it. This gave militant blacks a reason to label King a sellout.

Impatience turned violent, and riots broke out in major urban areas across the country through 1967. In a single week, violence erupted in as many as forty cities, including Detroit, Michigan. The Detroit riot was the worst race riot in American history up to that point. It started after police raided a nightclub and arrested seventy-five African American patrons. When news of these arrests spread, stores were looted and destroyed with fire-bombs. The riot lasted for four days. Thirty-eight people were dead and damage was estimated at

A National Guardsman readies his rifle at a Detroit intersection during the summer riots of 1967. African Americans erupted with frustration and despair when they saw little change in segregation policies following the Voting Rights Act of 1965.

$500 million. President Lyndon Johnson noted, "We have endured a week such as no nation should live through: a time of violence and tragedy."

The Assassin

The violence that had erupted on American streets, often referred to as race riots, continued into 1968. That same year, violence also claimed the life of Dr. Martin Luther King Jr. At the time of the shooting, a team of twelve Memphis police officers and county deputies were in and around Fire Station No. 2, down the street from the Lorraine Motel. After King was shot, the police officers raced to the motel. Other police officers quickly joined in and searched the area around the motel, as well as the buildings on South Main Street.

Minutes after the shooting, a deputy sheriff entered Jim's Grill. Inside, bartender and owner Loyd Jowers stood behind the counter serving nearly a dozen customers. Law enforcement officers spoke with Jowers that evening and several times over the next few days.

The Bundle

Within minutes of the assassination, police found a bundle on the sidewalk in front of Canipe's record store. It contained a Remington 30.06 rifle with a spent cartridge casing in its chamber, an attached scope, unfired Remington 30.06 ammunition, and items belonging to James Earl Ray. Ray's fingerprints were on the rifle and scope.

Firearms testing could not positively determine whether the fatal shot was or was not fired from the rifle recovered in front of Canipe's. The markings on the bullet removed from Dr. King's body, however, matched the general rifling characteristics of the discarded 30.06 rifle.

James Earl Ray

The man who many people believe shot Martin Luther King Jr. was a small-time crook and drifter who had escaped from prison. For much of his adult life, James Earl Ray had survived by robbing gas stations and stores. Ray left Memphis and drove to Atlanta, where he abandoned his Mustang the day after the assassination. Several days later, the Federal Bureau of Investigation (FBI)

The FBI issued this flyer when it placed the name of James Earl Ray on its list of the Ten Most Wanted Fugitives on April 20, 1968.

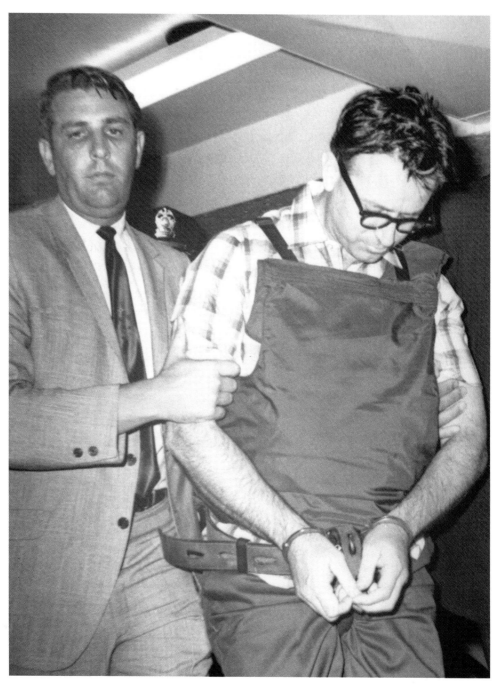

James Earl Ray, in handcuffs and with his head bowed, is led to his cell by Shelby County sheriff William Morris on July 19, 1968.

seized and searched the Mustang. At the time, Donald Wilson, a new special agent in the FBI's Atlanta office, participated in the search.

After abandoning the Mustang, Ray fled to Canada, where he had traveled the previous year after his escape from prison. Following a massive search, law enforcement officers arrested Ray in London, England, two months after the assassination.

In March 1969, Ray pled guilty to murdering Dr. King. When he entered his plea, he stated that he had purchased the 30.06 rifle; parked his Mustang just south of Canipe's (between Canipe's and Fire Station No. 2); shot Dr. King from the second floor bathroom of the rooming house; ran from the rooming house to his Mustang and dropped the rifle and other items in the bundle in front of Canipe's; and left the scene in his Mustang. Ray was sentenced to serve ninety-nine years in prison.

Ray Recants

Three days after pleading guilty, and for the next thirty years until his death in April 1998, James Earl Ray repeatedly attempted to withdraw his plea and obtain a new trial. Ray continually filed motions and separate lawsuits in both state and federal court. He claimed that his plea was involuntary, that he was denied a lawyer, that he was imprisoned illegally, and that he was not the assassin. Ray claimed that a mysterious man with Central Intelligence Agency (CIA) and Mafia (organized crime) contacts named "Raoul" or "Raul" had framed him. The authorities did not believe Ray, since he was unable to offer evidence to support his new claims. However, by denying his guilt, Ray sparked a controversy. Was Ray framed? Did he act alone?

Ray persistently maintained that he was innocent and that he was not at the rooming house when the fatal shot was fired. Ray argued that Raoul had not only planned the assassination but also made it look as if Ray was the shooter. But investigators felt that Ray had failed to provide a clear and believable

James Earl Ray testifies before the House of Representatives' Assassinations Committee in Washington, D.C., on August 16, 1978. Ray told the panel he did not kill Martin Luther King Jr.

description of his activities with Raoul prior to the assassination, or offer any evidence to support his claims.

In 1994, Ray filed the last of his several state petitions for a new trial. He based this request on his claim that the Remington 30.06 rifle, which the police discovered on South Main Street, was not the murder weapon. Additional firearms identification testing conducted to see if Ray's claim was true proved inconclusive. The petition was still pending in April 1998, when Ray died in prison.

Over the years, parties other than Ray have filed additional lawsuits related to the assassination. Most recently, after Ray's death in 1998, King family members filed a complaint in Tennessee state court charging Loyd Jowers with participating in a plot that resulted in the assassination of Dr. King.

A supervisory forensic scientist at the U.S. Fish and Wildlife Service Forensics Laboratory in Ashland, Oregon, uses an electron microscope to compare markings on two bullets in this December 1996 photo. The microscope is one of two in the United States that can conduct new tests on the rifle believed to have killed Martin Luther King Jr. This was done because James Earl Ray sought new evidence for a new murder trial.

Conspiracy Theories

Over the years, people have proposed a number of theories as to who really killed Martin Luther King Jr. Even those who witnessed the shooting disagree as to where the shot that killed King originated. Some stated that the shot did not come from the direction of Ray's boardinghouse room window. These disagreements have only fueled the debate. Just as with the assassination of President John F. Kennedy, some people suspect that powerful people organized a conspiracy, or plot, to murder Dr. King.

The FBI

King had many enemies, and throughout his life he was repeatedly threatened. Some people believe that government officials planned the King assassination. These people point out that government agents, especially those working for the FBI, hounded and harassed King. During his civil rights campaigns, King had verbally attacked the FBI for failing to protect civil rights workers in the South from violence. King's criticism angered FBI chief J. Edgar Hoover.

Hoover once described King as "the most dangerous man in America, and a moral degenerate." Under Hoover, the FBI used dirty tactics, such as secretly following King, tapping his phone and recording his conversations, and breaking into and entering his home and hotel rooms. They harassed not only King but also Malcolm X and countless other black activists during the civil rights struggle.

Reopening the Investigation

Suspicion surrounding FBI involvement in King's assassination was so strong that in 1977 the House Select Committee on Assassinations opened an investigation. From 1977 to 1978, the House committee investigated the assassination with a budget of almost $2.8 million and a staff of over 100 people. Much of the information compiled in that investigation was not released to the public. The committee did reveal that although the investigation uncovered shocking details of J. Edgar Hoover's efforts to discredit King, they found no evidence linking Hoover or the FBI to the assassination. James Earl Ray argued that if the committee released this information to the public, it would prove his innocence.

In 1997, one of Dr. King's sons, Dexter, visited James Earl Ray in the facility where Ray was being treated for terminal liver cancer. He asked Ray, "Did you kill my father?" Ray replied, "No, I didn't. No."

Dexter King *(left)*, son of slain civil rights leader Martin Luther King Jr., says good-bye to James Earl Ray, the man who confessed to killing King in 1969, following their meeting in Nashville, Tennessee, on March 27, 1997.

"I believe you and my family believes you," Dexter King said. The King family had come to believe that, indeed, there had been a conspiracy to kill Dr. King.

In August 1998, Attorney General Janet Reno decided that the family's doubts should not be ignored and ordered a new investigation into the assassination. The resulting Department of Justice investigation centered on two separate theories regarding the identity of King's assassin(s): the first by former FBI agent Donald Wilson, and the second by grill owner Loyd Jowers. Both men claimed to have evidence of a possible conspiracy to frame James Earl Ray for Dr. King's assassination.

Wilson and Jowers

In 1998, former FBI agent Donald Wilson claimed to have found a number of papers in Ray's abandoned white Mustang that suggested a conspiracy—evidence Wilson had concealed for thirty years. Wilson produced only a few pieces of paper with handwritten names and numbers, including the name Raul. However, Department of Justice investigators found that Wilson told inconsistent stories. They were also unable to find any other evidence to support his claim that the papers he possessed were originally in the Mustang or had any connection to James Earl Ray.

Earlier, in 1993, Loyd Jowers (the owner of the bar located below the rooming house across from the Lorraine Motel) said someone involved with the Mafia gave him $100,000 to hire an assassin. This person also assured him Memphis police would not be near the motel during the time of the shooting. Jowers claimed that someone whose name sounded like "Raoul" gave him a gun. He also claimed that the assassin fired from behind the tavern, not from the bathroom window in the rooming house.

Although Jowers told his story under oath, he later changed this version. As with Wilson's story, the Department of Justice found his story to be inconsistent and lacking in supporting evidence. Furthermore, during the original investigation, no footprints were found in the muddy ground behind the bar. (Jowers died in May 2000.)

Nevertheless, King's family believed Jowers's story, and in December 1997 sued him for wrongful death. A civil court jury concluded that Jowers and others, "including government agencies," conspired to assassinate King. It was in part because of this verdict that Janet Reno reopened the investigation in 1998.

Ultimately, the 1998 investigation rejected the findings of the civil case and the claims of Wilson and Jowers. "At this time we are aware of no information to warrant any further investigation of the assassination of Dr. Martin Luther King Jr.," the Department of Justice said. However, with the death of James Earl Ray in 1998 and the King family's continuing quest for the truth, the details of King's assassination remain a mystery.

America After King

On April 4, 1968, a campaign rally had been planned in Chicago for Senator Robert Kennedy, the brother of slain president John F. Kennedy. It was part of a national campaign tour for his bid for the 1968 Democratic nomination for the presidency. Just after his flight from Indianapolis, Indiana, Kennedy was informed of Martin Luther King Jr.'s death. Fearing a riot in response to the news of King's murder, police advised Kennedy not to make the planned stop, which was in a poor African American neighborhood. Kennedy, however, insisted on going.

When he arrived, he was greeted by an upbeat crowd. Everyone was excited about Kennedy's appearance. He climbed onto the platform, and realizing that the audience did not know about the assassination, he broke the news.

"I have bad news for you," he said, "for all of our fellow citizens, and people who love peace all over the world, and that is that Martin Luther King was shot and killed tonight." The crowd was stunned into silence. He continued, "Martin Luther King dedicated his life to love and to justice for his fellow human beings, and he died because of that effort."

Mourners view King's body before his funeral at Ebenezer Baptist Church in Atlanta, Georgia.

President Lyndon Johnson declared the day after King's assassination, April 5, 1968, a national day of mourning and ordered the United States flag to be flown at half-staff.

The Funeral

King's body was returned to Atlanta, where he was buried after a nationally televised funeral march on April 9, 1968. The Ebenezer Baptist Church, where his funeral was held, was surrounded by nearly 100,000 mourners. Inside the church were many powerful people, including politicians, civil rights activists, and entertainers.

In Memory of Dr. King

The following is an excerpt from Senator Robert Kennedy's speech in Chicago on April 4, 1968:

We can move in that direction as a country, in greater polarization—black people amongst blacks, and white amongst whites, filled with hatred toward one another. Or we can make an effort, as Martin Luther King did, to understand and to comprehend, and replace that violence, that stain of bloodshed that has spread across our land, with an effort to understand with compassion and love.

For those of you who are black and are tempted to be filled with hatred and mistrust of the injustice of such an act, against all white people, I would only say that I can also feel in my own heart the same kind of feeling. I had a member of my family killed, but he was killed by a white man.

But we have to make an effort in the United States, we have to make an effort to understand, to get beyond these rather difficult times. So I ask you tonight to return home, to say a prayer for the family of Martin Luther King, that's true, but more importantly to say a prayer for our own country, which all of us love—a prayer for understanding and that compassion of which I spoke. The vast majority of white people and the vast majority of black people in this country want to live together, want to improve the quality of our life, and want justice for all human beings that abide in our land.

Let us dedicate ourselves to what the Greeks wrote so many years ago: to tame the savageness of man and make gentle the life of this world.

Martin Luther King Jr.'s funeral procession winds down West
Hunter Street in Atlanta, Georgia.

Reverend Ralph Abernathy succeeded Dr. King as
president of the SCLC. He completed his friend's
vision of a Poor People's Campaign march in June
1968. Although vandalism and violence marred the
march, it was a success. Over 50,000 people
marched a mile to show legislators how many
people live in wretched poverty.

The Nation Reacts

In spite of King's lifelong position against violence, and in spite of the efforts of black leaders to calm his followers, violence broke out after the assassination.

Rioting occurred in more than 100 cities around the country, including Memphis, Baltimore, Pittsburgh, and Chicago. Seattle residents hurled firebombs, broke windows, and pelted motorists with rocks. Some 10,000 people marched to Seattle Center for a rally in memory of Dr. King. The government called in over 68,000 soldiers to help stop the violence. It is estimated that more than 20,000 people were arrested and over $45 million in property was destroyed. At least forty African Americans and five whites were killed.

After the assassination of Martin Luther King Jr., rioting broke out in more than 100 cities around the United States, including Memphis, Baltimore, Pittsburgh, and Chicago.

For the general population of whites, King's assassination brought feelings of guilt and shame. They reacted to it by donating money to the SCLC in record amounts. On April 10, Congress passed the 1968 Civil Rights Act, which curbed discrimination in housing. It is often described as a tribute to King.

King's Legacy

King's death has had an impact on the direction of social change in America. His assassination, along with those of President John F. Kennedy and his brother Senator Robert F. Kennedy, became a national obsession, spawning conspiracy theories and reopening investigations. It is often said that the hopes and dreams of millions of Americans died with these men.

As a prominent leader of the civil rights movement, Martin Luther King Jr. not only stirred African Americans into action, he also reached the hearts and minds of white Americans. During Martin Luther King Jr.'s lifetime, the rising tide of civil rights activity influenced public opinion and led to the passage of important civil rights legislation, including the Civil Rights Act of 1964, followed by the 1965 passage of the Voting Rights Act.

Changing the Future

King changed the future for many Americans, including that of his friend and close associate Reverend Jesse Jackson. In 1984 and in 1988, Jackson, who was nearby when King was assassinated, became the first African American to make a serious bid for president of the United States.

Today, the discrimination faced by racial minorities at the time King began his crusade is to some degree a shadow of the past. Public facilities are no longer segregated. Laws protect the rights of all citizens to equal opportunity for employment, housing, and the right to vote. However, most agree that equality for all citizens is still a work in progress. In spite of the civil rights victories achieved by King and other civil rights activists, his dream of equality for racial minorities continues to face new setbacks.

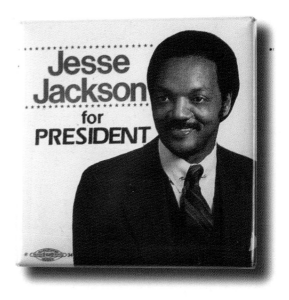

Jesse Jackson has fought for the rights of all Americans through his Rainbow Coalition. He also ran for president in 1984 and 1988.

As recently as April 12, 2001, the anniversary of King's imprisonment in Birmingham, a citywide curfew was imposed in Cincinnati, Ohio. It followed demonstrations, which were peaceful during the day but which disintegrated into looting, arson, and random shootings at night. This began after police shot an unarmed African American man to death during an attempted arrest on April 7. He was the fifth African American man killed by city police in seven months. The NAACP responded to the crisis by calling for a town meeting.

In His Own Words

Not long before he died, King described how he would like to be remembered in his autobiography, *The Autobiography of Martin Luther King, Jr.*:

I'd like someone to mention that day that Martin Luther King, Jr., tried to give his life serving others. I'd like somebody to say that day that Martin Luther King, Jr., tried to love somebody. I want you to be able to say that day that I did try to feed the hungry. I want you to be able to say that day that I did try in my life to clothe the naked. I want you to say on that day that I did try in my life to visit those who were in prison. And I want you to say that I tried to love and serve humanity.

King's family, headed by his wife, Coretta Scott King, carries on his legacy. After his death, she became a civil rights leader in her own right, campaigning for human rights, social justice, and programs to improve housing and living conditions in cities. She founded the Martin Luther King Jr. Center for Nonviolent Social Change in Atlanta, Georgia, which is dedicated to training people in nonviolent social protest. In 1995, her son, Dexter, replaced her as the center's president and chief executive officer. She has also established the annual Coretta Scott King Award to honor outstanding African American authors of children's books.

A National Holiday

In 1986, thanks especially to the efforts of Coretta Scott King, Dr. King's birthday, January 15, became a federal holiday. On this day, banks, the stock market, the United States Postal Service, and many government offices close each year. In 1992, every state had approved some form of the holiday, although ironically, in some southern states, King must share the day with Civil War Confederate general Robert E. Lee.

In 2001, on what would have been King's seventy-second birthday, the nation celebrated Dr. King with speeches, services, and parades. As he left office, President Bill Clinton addressed an audience of 900 at the University of the District of Columbia's King Day celebration. He called for social and political changes to address continuing racial problems in the United States.

King is a hero to activists pursuing equal rights for all citizens. In August 2000, on the thirty-seventh anniversary of the March on Washington and his "I Have a Dream" speech, thousands rallied along the Capitol Mall, following in the footsteps of Dr. Martin Luther King Jr. They called for an end to the racial profiling (a practice in which police stop a suspect based on the color of his or her skin) and police brutality that many say are keeping that dream from becoming a reality.

Marchers celebrate the birthday of Martin Luther King Jr. on January 18, 1999, in Seattle, Washington.

Among these activists was Dr. King's son Martin Luther King III, who stated, "My father stood not far from here, trying to redeem the soul of America. I challenge you to ensure that he did not die in vain." While Martin Luther King Jr.'s struggle for social justice was halted by violence, we all share the fruits of his legacy. We also share the responsibility to make the dream of a truly democratic United States a reality.

Changing Times

1954
The Supreme Court issues its decision in *Brown v. Board of Education*, declaring segregation of public schools illegal.

1957
Martin Luther King Jr. is elected president of the SCLC.

1960
John F. Kennedy is elected president of the United States.

1961
Freedom rides to protest segregation in transportation begin.

1962
John Glenn orbits the globe in a space capsule.

1963
President John F. Kennedy is assassinated; Lyndon Johnson becomes president.

1964
The Economic Opportunity Act allocates funds to fight poverty.

July 1964
The Civil Rights Act is signed into law.

November 1964
Johnson is elected president.

The Assassination of Martin Luther King Jr.

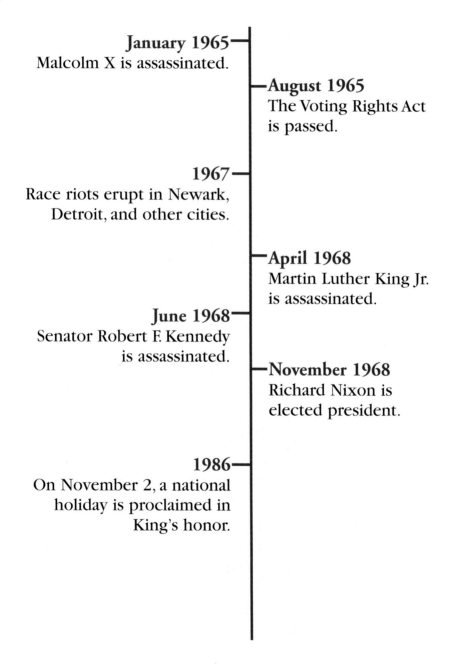

January 1965
Malcolm X is assassinated.

August 1965
The Voting Rights Act
is passed.

1967
Race riots erupt in Newark,
Detroit, and other cities.

April 1968
Martin Luther King Jr.
is assassinated.

June 1968
Senator Robert F. Kennedy
is assassinated.

November 1968
Richard Nixon is
elected president.

1986
On November 2, a national
holiday is proclaimed in
King's honor.

Glossary

advocate To speak in support of a person or a cause.

arson Malicious, illegal burning of property.

assassination Murder by sudden or secret attack, usually for impersonal reasons.

black separatism Belief in or movement for the creation of a separate black nation.

class Group sharing the same economic conditions.

constitution Basic principles and laws of a nation that determine the powers and duties of the government and guarantee rights to the people in it.

constitutional Relating to or being in agreement with the constitution of a nation.

controversy Discussion about a question over which there is strong disagreement.

demonstration Public display of group feelings toward a person or a cause.

discredit To destroy confidence in a person or a cause.

discrimination Unjust difference in the way a person or group is treated as compared with another.

dissent To differ in opinion.

dissenter One who dissents.

injunction   Court order whereby one is required to do something or refrain from doing something.

integration   The act of incorporating a smaller group into a larger unit.

legislation   The laws that are made.

militant   Aggressively active.

momentum   Strength or force gained by motion or a series of events.

movement   Series of acts working toward a desired end.

oppress   To crush or burden by abuse of power.

practical   Of or relating to practice and action; useful.

prejudice   Favoring or disliking one over another without good reason.

resistance   Opposing force.

segregation   Separation or isolation by acts of discrimination, such as of a race.

sit-in   Act of sitting as a means of organized protest.

surveillance   Close watch kept over someone or something.

white supremacist   One who believes in a white race and a black race and, further, that the white race is naturally superior.

For More Information

Center for Law and Social Policy
1616 P Street NW, Suite 150
Washington, DC 20036
(202) 328-5140
Web site: http://www.clasp.org

Human and Civil Rights Organizations of America
408 F Street NE
Washington, DC 20002
(202) 547-4105
Web site: http://www.hcr.org

Martin Luther King Jr. Papers Project
Cypress Hall D-Wing
Stanford University
Stanford, CA 94305-4146
Web site: http://www.stanford.edu/groups/King

National Civil Rights Museum
The Lorraine Motel
450 Mulberry Street
Memphis, TN 38103-4214

(901) 521-9699
Web site: http://www.civilrightsmuseum.org

Poverty and Race Research Action Council
3000 Connecticut Avenue NW, Suite 200
Washington, DC 20008
(202) 387-9887
Web site: http://www.prrac.org

Videos

Eyes on the Prize: America's Civil Rights Years, 1954-1965. Blackside Films, 1987.

Eyes on the Prize II: America at the Racial Crossroads, 1965-1985. Blackside Films, 1989.

Web Sites

The Martin Luther King Jr. Center for Nonviolent Social Change
http://www.thekingcenter.com

The Martin Luther King Jr. Papers Project
http://www.stanford.edu/group/King

The National Association for the Advancement of Colored People
http://www.naacp.org

For Further Reading

Adler, David A. *A Picture Book of Dr. Martin Luther King, Jr.* New York: Holiday House, 1991.

Cone, James H. *Martin and Malcolm and America: A Dream or a Nightmare.* Mary Knoll, NY: Orbis Books, 1991.

King, Coretta Scott. *My Life with Martin Luther King, Jr.* New York: Puffin, 1993.

King, Martin Luther, Jr. *Why We Can't Wait.* New York: Signet Classic, 2000.

King, Martin Luther, Jr., and Coretta Scott King. *The Words of Martin Luther King Jr.* 2nd ed. New York: Newmarket Press, 2001.

Lane, Mark, and Dick Gregory. *Murder in Memphis: The FBI and the Assassination of Martin Luther King.* New York: Thunder's Mouth Press, 1993.

Moses, Greg. *Revolution of Conscience.* New York: Guilford Press, 1996.

Oates, Stephen B. *Let the Trumpet Sound: A Life of Dr. Martin Luther King, Jr.* New York: Harperperennial Library, 1997.

Posner, Gerald. *Killing the Dream: James Earl Ray and the Assassination of Martin Luther King, Jr.* San Diego, CA: Harvest Books, 1999.

Index

Index

About the Author

Jacqueline Ching is a New York-based writer and editor who has written for the *Seattle Times* and *Newsweek* magazine. This is her seventh book for the Rosen Publishing Group.

Photo Credits

Cover and pp. 4, 21, 23, 26, 35, 36, 38, 46 © Bettmann/Corbis; pp. 1, 10, 11, 13, 15, 19, 25, 33, 54 © AP/Photo World Wide; pp. 16, 28, 49, 51 © Timepix; p. 29 © Flip Schulke/Corbis; p. 39 © AP/*Ashland Daily Tidings*; p. 42 © AP/The State of Tennessee; p. 48 © James Amoa/Corbis.

Series Design and Layout

Les Kanturek